The Way of Pilgrimage is like a new best friend! You can walk right into its welcoming presence and begin at once to find fresh truths sprouting up from ancient sources. It will become a trusted guide for those who accompany youth and young adults on their paths of meaning-making.

It promises especially satisfying moments for leaders who wish to engage others in the rhythmic paces of spiritual formation. The weekly gatherings show us how to move from deeply ingrained habits of content-based Bible study into soul-tending practices of contemplation and community that open us to transformation.

—The Reverend Dr. Dori Baker
Author, *Doing Girlfriend Theology: God-Talk with Young Women*
United Methodist pastor and professor of youth ministry and Christian education

As an organization completely dedicated to the art of pilgrimage, we are overjoyed with *The Way of Pilgrimage* resources. *The Way of Pilgrimage* is a comprehensive and passionate guide that brings us back to our ancient heritage of pilgrimage through modern eyes and practical application.

Utilize these resources to teach your youth God's unique design of our lives as journeys of exploration and adventure. There is no better resource available to date that prepares your teens as lifelong pilgrims.

—Shawn Small
Executive director, Wonder Voyage Pilgrimages

Finally—a spiritual resource for youth and young adults with depth and meaning! Upper Room Books continues its Companions in Christ series with an insightful and creative journey for Generation Next. I love this resource!

—Bo Prosser
Coordinator for congregational life, Cooperative Baptist Fellowship

This inspiring resource seeks its participants out wherever they are in their spiritual walks and gently moves them toward a deeper understanding of their own pilgrimage. In the context of a Christian community of travelers, participants shed light on the most unexamined corners of their souls. . . .

As an educator of secondary students, I greatly appreciate how consistently this text works to provide spiritual development activities for every kind of learner—from still meditation to verbal expression to artistic interpretations.

—Jessica Rosenthal
United Methodist educator and youth helper

The Way of Pilgrimage is a wonderful doorway into the spiritual life. Like the bountiful feast that God sets before us, these volumes are full of wisdom and blessing. Those who accept the challenge to walk with Christ would benefit greatly from this guide. Its exercises are both simple and rich. At every point, the members of the group are encouraged to journey into the heart of God.

—The Reverend Daniel Wolpert
Pastor, First Presbyterian Church, Crookston, Minnesota
Codirector, Minnesota Institute of Contemplation and Healing (MICAH)
Author, *Leading a Life with God*

STEPPING INTO THE WORLD

PARTICIPANT'S BOOK

Kara Lassen Oliver

VOLUME **5**

UPPER ROOM BOOKS®

NASHVILLE

STEPPING INTO THE WORLD
Participant's Book Volume 5
Copyright © 2007 by Upper Room Books
All rights reserved.
The Upper Room® Web site: http://www.upperroom.org

At the time of publication all Web sites referenced in this book were valid. However, due to the fluid nature of the Internet some addresses may have changed or the content may no longer be relevant.

Cover design: Left Coast Design, Portland, OR
Interior design: Gore Studio, Inc., Nashville, TN
Typesetting: PerfecType, Nashville, TN
First printing: 2007

ISBN-13   978-0-8358-9838-6
ISBN-10   0-8358-9838-5

LIBRARY OF CONGRESS CATALOGING-IN-PUBLICATION DATA
OLIVER, KARA.
  Stepping into the world : participant's book / Kara Lassen Oliver.
    p. cm. — (The way of pilgrimage ; v. 5)
  Includes bibliographical references.
  1. Christian youth—Religious life. 2. Vocation—Christianity. 3. Spiritual formation. I. Oliver, Kara. Way of pilgrimage. II. Title.
  BV4531.3.O42 2007
  263'.041—dc22   2007003692

Printed in the United States of America

CONTENTS

MEET THE WRITER

Kara Lassen Oliver has been working with and learning from young people for the past eight years. While working on her Master of Divinity at Vanderbilt Divinity School she worked at the United Methodist Youth Organization. Then feeling a call to the local church she served as Youth Pastor at Belmont United Methodist Church for three years. Now with two children she enjoys more time at home while working part-time as a writer. Along with her husband, Jeff, and her kids, Claire Marin and Carter, they live and worship and play in Nashville, Tennessee.

ACKNOWLEDGMENTS

The Way of Pilgrimage is a new adventure in spiritual formation for a new generation of Companions in Christ groups. The original twenty-eight-week *Companions in Christ* resource was published by Upper Room Books in spring 2001. The ensuing Companions in Christ series has been designed to create settings in which people can respond to God's call to an ever-deepening communion and wholeness in Christ—as individuals, as members of a small group, and as part of a congregation. Building upon the *Companions in Christ* foundational vision, *The Way of Pilgrimage* is written for a younger audience of senior high youth and first-year college students.

The first consultation for developing *The Way of Pilgrimage* took place in Nashville in February 2005. We are deeply grateful to these consultants and to the writers of the Leader's Guide and Participant's Books: Sally Chambers, Kyle Dugan, Steve Matthews, Craig Mitchell, Jeremy Myers, Jonathon Norman, Kara Lassen Oliver, Gavin Richardson, Ciona Rouse, Jessica Rosenthal, Daniel Wolpert, and Jenny Youngman. Special thanks to Stephen Bryant, visionary leader of the Companions in Christ resources and publisher of Upper Room Ministries. He developed and wrote all the daily exercises found in this book.

We are also indebted to those who reviewed the early manuscript and offered their insights on theology and pilgrimage: The Reverend Matthew Corkern, Christ Church Cathedral Episcopal Church in Nashville, Tennessee; Sally Chambers, St. Paul's Episcopal Church in Franklin, Tennessee; and Jeremy Myers, Augsburg College in Minneapolis, Minnesota.

The following churches and groups tested portions of early versions of *The Way of Pilgrimage*:

- Belmont United Methodist Church in Nashville, Tennessee (leader: Jessica Rosenthal)
- Wesley United Methodist Church in Coral Gables, Florida (leader: the Reverend César J. Villafaña)

- First United Methodist Church in Hendersonville, Tennessee (leader: Gavin Richardson)
- North Park University in Chicago, Illinois (leaders: Susan Braun and Jodi DeYoung)
- Milford United Methodist Church in Milford, Michigan (leader: Sherry Foster)
- Westminster Presbyterian Church in Eugene, Oregon (leaders: Jen Butler and Katie Stocks)
- St. Paul's Episcopal Church in Richmond, Virginia (leader: Steve Matthews)
- SoulFeast 2006 Youth Program in Lake Junaluska, North Carolina (leader: Ciona Rouse)

The Companions in Christ Staff Team
Upper Room Ministries

INTRODUCTION

You have made us for yourself, O Lord,
and our heart is restless till it rests in you.

—Saint Augustine

We are a pilgrim people, always moving, always wanting more, never satisfied, never full, and never finished. We are a pilgrim people.

Throughout the scriptures, God continually reminds us of our pilgrim hearts and calls us back to the path that leads us home. The psalmist declares, "For I am . . . a traveler passing through, as my ancestors were before me" (Ps. 39:12, NLT). And the letter to the Hebrews says it quite simply: We are "strangers and pilgrims on the earth" (11:13, NKJV). The word *pilgrim* comes from the Latin word meaning "resident alien." This world is not our home. Our life here on earth is just one stop on this all-encompassing pilgrimage, a physical and spiritual journey home to the One to whom we truly belong. We *are* a pilgrim people.

In your hands you hold the map for a six-week pilgrimage: a journey in which we seek the God who made us, redeemed us, and still walks with us; a journey that leads us back home into the heart of God. On this journey we practice outwardly ways to mark the inner journey, the journey of our hearts. And though it is an inward journey, God calls each of us to carry this journey outward into the world.

On pilgrimage we hear the risen Christ calling to us. He called us to pilgrimage in the first place, and he continues to call our name as we walk to him. God calls each of us to be a radical, vulnerable, and available pilgrim in and to this world. Let's face it, the world needs more pilgrims! God needs more people to remember who they are: to remember that they are pilgrims.

On pilgrimage we begin to uncover God's purpose and greater calling is to each of us. God gives us gifts that enable us answer the call, and mission and purpose to help direct us on our journey. And most importantly, God calls each of us Beloved. So now we each face the question of how to step out into the world, continue our journey, as the pilgrim God has made and called. We may echo T. S. Eliot's poem "Little Gidding" when our journey concludes, finding we come back home and "know the place for the first time."[1] Pilgrimage is not about escaping the world but coming face-to-face with the reality of the world and the reality of our hearts. It's about leaving home to find home: to find our place in this world as we find our dwelling in God. Before we begin, here are a few reminders for the road:

There is a difference between being a tourist and being a pilgrim.

Just as we can travel to holy places as a tourist, not fully engaged or fully present, we also can walk this spiritual pilgrimage of faith as a tourist. Tourists may take snapshots of places along the way and yet still keep their hearts far removed, offering empty words to those they meet. Tourists also may be here only for the community and not the journey. *This is a journey for pilgrims.*

Companions along the way are essential to pilgrimage.

Keep in mind that even though we travel with others, each pilgrim must make his or her own journey. As fellow pilgrims we journey side by side, looking out together for the One we seek.

Each weekly gathering is a stop along the way.

Each gathering is space carved out and made holy. When we gather together, the gateway between God and us seems wider, and the intersection of heaven and earth more apparent. Each gathering is a place that says, *Welcome, pilgrims. Welcome to this respite. Welcome to this holy place.*

Rhythm is part of our daily routine as pilgrims.

In medieval times, pilgrims would set out on their journey in exactly the same way. Ritual and repetition were intrinsic to pilgrimage. And because pilgrims followed the same path, we can follow medieval pilgrim trails today in Europe and in the Holy Land. Every Good Friday pilgrims walk the way of the cross, the same path Jesus walked to his death (according to tradition). The repetition and rhythm of the daily exercises and readings are essential to this participant's book. So stick with them, and you will find that particular prayers, scriptures, and practices that are repeated through our journey will begin to sink from your head down to your heart; they will become as familiar and comforting as wearing a favorite old pair of shoes.

Pilgrimage is about being present in the present.

This pilgrimage is about waking up and paying attention to our lives. It also involves remembering our past. As we live our days awake to God in prayer, we will become present to God and to life.

This is a journey of the heart as well as the head.

In this journey, prayer, conversation, listening, reading, noticing, and looking are transformed from activities of the mind to practices of the heart.

You are invited to engage in the exercises each day and read the daily readings. The shaded paragraphs you'll find in the readings offer an essential idea in the passage. Be sure to get yourself a journal to use for exercises, reflections, and group meetings.

So welcome, pilgrim! May you journey faithfully and with integrity. May you make great strides, though this pilgrimage does not literally go far. As you learn to listen for the word of God, allowing it to guide you on this way, may you come to know who you really are and what you truly seek. And may Christ "dwell in your hearts through faith, as you are being rooted and grounded in love. . . . May [you] have the power to comprehend, with all the saints, what is the breadth and length and height and depth, and to know the love of Christ that surpasses knowledge, so that you may be filled with all the fullness of God" (Eph. 3:17-19).

Welcome home. Welcome to *The Way of Pilgrimage.*

—Sally Chambers
Coauthor, *The Way of Pilgrimage* Leader's Guide

The story of Moses provides clear illustrations of a man called even from birth by God. He did not hear the call until later in life, and even then he was hesitant to follow; yet God chose him and was with him throughout his life. Listening carefully to his story can help us refocus on where we are hearing God's call in our lives. What are you hearing God calling you to be and do? Set aside ten to fifteen minutes each day to do the exercises this week. Use your journal to note your thoughts as you do them.

CALLED FROM BIRTH

Day 1 Exercise

READ EXODUS 1:15–2:10.

REFLECT Our personal calling begins with our personal creation, God's calling us forth to life on earth. Moses' story shows the secret ways God saved Moses and the unseen ways God was saving the suffering Israelites through the faithfulness of certain people.

Where do you see evidence of God's care and saving purpose in the story of Moses' birth? Where do you see evidence of God's care and purpose in the story of how you came to be?

PRAY "For it was you who formed my inward parts; you knit me together in my mother's womb. I praise you, for I am fearfully and wonderfully made" (Ps. 139:13-14a). Make this prayer your own today. Contemplate the mystery of your being and all the little things over time that led to the reality of your being here.

ACT Notice the mystery of each person you are with today and the possibility that God called each one into being for a purpose.

Day 1 Reading

Our story and our calling begin at our beginning. Our parents, whether biological or adoptive, have cared for and shaped us even before our birth. This was true for Jesus also, especially in relation to his mother, Mary.

Let's overhear an imaginative account of Mary's thoughts as she considers the child within her and how she will participate in his life. We can learn a lot from her faith and her joy in moments of uncertainty.

Walking the dusty road, I shook my head and wondered where my bold words had come from. As odd as it may seem, it was not so much seeing an angel that caused the knot in my stomach but the way I spoke to the angel. Did I really question a messenger of God? As badly as I want to pretend it didn't happen, I did indeed ask, "How can this be?" I should be thankful God did not strike me down right then. Instead, the angel patiently explained the unexplainable, that I will bear a child, although I have never been with a man, not even with my fiancé, Joseph.

Joseph! What will he say? What will he do? I can't think of that now. I have to trust in God.

At least I regained my wits soon enough to assure the angel that I am a faithful servant of the Lord, ready to do as the Lord asks. But a "Son of God"? What does that mean?

I decided I must go to my cousin Elizabeth. But how would I explain why I came? Should I tell her about my strange visitor? I wondered whether she and Zechariah would let me stay. I was approaching their house, and before I could make any decisions, the door burst open. Elizabeth cried out, "Blessed are you among women, and blessed is the fruit of your womb. And why has this happened to me, that the mother of my Lord comes to me? For as soon as I heard the sound of your greeting, the child in my womb leaped for joy. And blessed is she who believed that there would be a fulfillment of what was spoken to her by the Lord" (Luke 1:42-45).

My knees grew weak, and the rest of my doubts fled before I kneeled. I could only say, "My soul magnifies the Lord, and my spirit rejoices in God my Savior, for he has looked with favor on the lowliness of his servant. Surely, from now on all generations will call me blessed; for the Mighty One has done great things for me, and holy is his name" (Luke 1:46-49).

CLAIMED IN OUR BAPTISM

Day 2 Exercise

READ EXODUS 1:15–2:10.

REFLECT The waters of baptism remind us that we are here because God chose each of us to share the life of Christ for the sake of others. In the story of Moses we read, "She named him Moses, 'because,' she said, 'I drew him out of water'" (Exod. 2:10).

Reflect on the ways God has drawn you, like Moses, "out of the water"—the waters of life that have borne you, have threatened you, or have saved you for something greater.

Sketch a basket going down a river with you in it. Behind the basket, name the blessings that have birthed you, carried you, and saved you for who you can be today. In front of the basket, name the dangers, challenges, and possibilities in the waters ahead of you.

PRAY Personalize the scripture, "I drew _(Your Name)_ out of the water." Hear God speaking to you. Express your gratitude. Ask for God's continued care and guidance on the river of life.

ACT Whenever you see water today, remember your baptism and the words, "I drew _(Your Name)_ out of the water."

Day 2 Reading

The baptismal font sits right in the middle of my home church sanctuary. When you walk down the center aisle, you have to detour around the font to get to the front of the church. My favorite place to sit in worship is within ten or twelve feet of that baptismal font. It's not because I like to be in the center of things or because my family always sits in the same pew. It's because when you open any of the hymnals within that twelve-foot radius, you find the pages warped and wrinkled from water spray.

In our church, after each baptism the pastors take handfuls of water and throw them out into the congregation. As water lands on the people, their Sunday dresses, silk ties, and hymnals, the words ring out, "Remember your baptism and be thankful!"

Through the act of baptism, both family and congregation claim that the baptized one is a child of God, beloved of God. We vow to pray for and to care for this infant, child, or adult as a member of our Christian family. And as the water falls again on those nearby, they can remember and reclaim their own belovedness in the family of God. As I sit in those pews I am reminded that I too have been baptized and am beloved of God. What a beautiful recollection on days when I feel less than lovable.

Hear the words from Mark 1:11: "*You* are my Son, the Beloved; with you I am well pleased"; and from Matt. 3:17: "*This* is my Son, the Beloved, with whom I am well pleased" (emphases added). Only one word changes. In Mark, God speaks directly and intimately to Jesus, assuring him, reminding him, that nothing can separate him from the love of God: "*You* are my Son." In Matthew, God publicly proclaims to all who can hear, so there will be no confusion: "*This* is my Son."

Whether you were baptized as a child or an adult or are still considering baptism; whether you have been sprinkled or dunked, you can be assured of these same proclamations, both intimate and quiet as well as public and resounding: "You are my child, the Beloved."

DAILY DECISIONS TO HONOR GOD'S CALL

Day 3 Exercise

READ EXODUS 2:11-22.

REFLECT A great preacher once said, "Character may be manifested in the great moments, but it is made in the small ones."[1] The story of Moses' young adulthood illustrates how our response to the small moments can shape us forever. We meet the great challenge of honoring God's call in the midst of everyday living.

Mark all the decisions Moses had to make in these verses. In each decision, consider the ways Moses honored his calling or did not. If you had been in Moses' shoes, where would you have struggled over what to do?

What decisions do you struggle with? What does it mean to honor God's call in the way you decide to respond?

PRAY When he arrives in Midian, Moses sits down by a well. Sit by the well of God's presence in prayer. Cup your hands and place any decision you struggle with into that well, as a way of offering the decision to God. After letting go, relax your hands; give God time with your decision as you rest and wait. After a few minutes of quiet, reach down into that imaginary well and let God give you back your challenge afresh. What is different? What's been added or subtracted?

ACT As you face each challenging situation today, pause, cup your hands as a quiet act of prayer, and think of what it means to honor God with all you think, say, and do.

Day 3   Reading

Have you ever received a piece of advice so valuable that you wrote it down and kept it in your wallet until you could barely read the worn writing anymore? But even then, just having the paper was enough, because you had memorized the advice long before the ink faded away. I received one of those pieces of wisdom at a point in my life when I was overcommitted, stressed out, and just plain crabby.

Over coffee with my Bible study leader, I explained my dilemma. I was involved in too many activities and had committed myself in too many places—but they were all good and valuable things to be doing. How could I figure out which commitments to continue and which to break? How could I know each day where to put my energies and focus my efforts?

My Bible study leader asked me to pay attention to my energy level after each activity. Thinking through my day, I soon realized (as she knew I would) that I felt more energy and excitement after activities where I had used my God-given gifts. After doing research or coaching gymnastics, I was energized and ready to go. After a long meeting or a group session with lots of people, I wanted to retreat to my room and take a nap.

My wise mentor had helped me to see that when I respond to God's authentic call, not only do I have more energy for the task but I also receive more energy in return. The longer I have lived with that advice tucked in my mental back pocket, the more clearly I recognize its wisdom. It holds true for major life decisions like what career to pursue and also for smaller and more frequent decisions, such as how to reply to my mom's phone call, which TV programs to watch, and whether I find time to read the Bible each day.

This is what following a calling means: making decisions each day to honor the gifts God has given us and paying attention to where God activates our energies and passions.

MULTIPLE CALLINGS IN LIFE

Day 4 Exercise

READ EXODUS 2:15–3:10.

REFLECT Our calling is not limited to specific occupations or activities; it is a journey guided by the voice of God's love leading us into the life for which we were made. In these verses, Moses faced the challenge of hearing God's call in the midst of multiple commitments.

List the commitments that define Moses' life in Exodus 2:15-22, imagining how he might have prioritized them.

What call does God introduce in 3:7-10, and how does it rearrange and redefine the other commitments in Moses' life?

PRAY Spend a few minutes mulling over the section 2:23-25. Ask God to help you see or feel a place where people today are groaning in bondage and crying out to God. Where do you perceive God hearing their groaning and remembering them in love?

ACT Learn more about a situation of human suffering that concerns you.

Day 4 Reading

Following God's call involves a delicate process of learning to be still and listen for promptings from the Holy Spirit. These promptings may warn us of poor decisions and lead us into the abundant life God desires for us. Following God's call does not mean we will always experience an easy or happy life. It does mean we will experience life fully and authentically. Our calling can—and probably will—change over the course of our life. A calling does not equate with a specific career, position, or project. Rather, it initiates a journey that leads us into new places, new communities, new challenges—and always into a truly meaningful life.

As a twelve-year-old in the Temple, Jesus knew he belonged in the house of his spiritual Father yet may have had little idea what his future vocation would actually involve. At some point Jesus probably became a carpenter, working and learning from his father, perhaps imagining this to be his life's work. Then, around the age of thirty, Jesus heard a new call—to baptism, to the desert, to temptation, and to a world-changing ministry. Was Jesus slow to hear his call, or was God progressively leading him into the fullness of his life's purpose, through a sequence of callings—son, student, carpenter, prophet . . . savior?

Some life paths seem to follow a natural and seamless progression. Others, like that of the apostle Paul, involve abrupt stops and drastic turns. Paul started down the Damascus road with a clear and fervent belief in his duty to persecute and kill Christians. When he heard God's true call on his life, he started down a very different path. He himself was persecuted and humbled, but his labors for Christ were immensely fruitful and joyful.

For us too our call may seem crystal clear today, yet tomorrow we may need to squint into the distance to discern where God is leading us. But we can be sure that all true callings from God will lead us into abundant life.

CALLED TOGETHER AT EVERY AGE

Day 5 Exercise

REVIEW EXODUS 2:15–3:6.

REFLECT God calls each of us but not each alone. God calls us to be the body of Christ *together,* in ways we could never be in ministry alone. Moses was able to respond to God's call as an individual because other people in his life had brought him to this place.

Make a list of all the people who played a role in the drama of Moses' life. Would Moses have been able to fulfill his calling without any one of them? Notice that one key player was quite young—Moses' own sister (Exod. 2:4, 8).

Think about your own life. What special concern has God put in your heart? Name some people who have played a role in your awareness and action around this concern, whatever their age.

PRAY Listen for God's call, not just for you alone but for you and some of your friends or your group. What is God calling any of you to do or be together for the sake of others that you could never do or be by yourself?

ACT Share any answer or insight with your group when you meet.

Day 5 Reading

During one season of Lent, a small Presbyterian church offered a light supper of soup and bread along with a Bible study each Wednesday night to help parishioners more fully understand Jesus' journey to the cross. A group of about eight people gathered each week in the fellowship hall to discuss and ask questions about the study.

The questions intrigued Grace the most. She loved to read scripture; the stories captivated her. And she always had questions after reading. The group was small enough and the people kind enough that even at age sixteen—the only teenager in the group—Grace didn't feel awkward asking her questions. Between bites of bread and slurps of soup, she would ask *why* and *how* and *what does that mean?* And the group would wrestle with the questions together.

After about three weeks, the craziest thing happened. As the group broke up for the evening, the leader asked Grace if she would like to lead the study the following week. Flattered and intimidated (but only a little), she said yes after a little prompting. She spent the week reading and preparing. The next week when she arrived, she had butterflies in her stomach, but she was ready. As the bread was passed, the soup served, and the scripture read, her anxiety passed. The group read and studied together as they had every other Wednesday.

Years later Grace could not recall what book they studied that Lent or even one question she asked in those meetings. But she can tell you that during that Lenten season she began to understand how the body of Christ includes all people and honors every person's gifts. A single invitation shaped her view of God and the church forever.

This week the exercises focus on practices that help us learn to listen to God in daily life. Listening for God's call and presence in our lives takes practice. And we have to keep listening to know where we are going. In a world of mixed messages, discerning God's voice requires some tools. Keep your journal close by this week to note your thoughts.

STILLNESS AND LISTENING

Day 1 Exercise

READ LUKE 4:42.

REFLECT Living God's call requires a listening way of life. We may picture Jesus as always *doing*—teaching, performing miracles, or changing the world in some way. But if we read carefully, we see that Jesus mixed his *doing* with times of *being* in "a deserted place," listening to God. (See also Luke 6:12 and 22:39.)

Seventeenth-century American Christian William Penn once wrote, "In the rush and noise of life, as you have intervals, step within yourselves and be still. Wait upon God and feel [God's] good presence; this will carry you through your day's business."[1]

Can you identify the intervals in the rush and noise of your life where you can be still? How might a few moments of silence each day change your outlook, stress level, or relationship with God?

PRAY "Step within" yourself now and be still. Do nothing but rest in God's presence.

ACT Find a few other moments to sit or walk in silence today.

Day 1 Reading

I once encountered a woman who wore stillness like a comfortable favorite sweater. When I first met her, I was running late—as usual—for a retreat. I came bustling into the room, still thinking about things left undone that morning, ready to explain why I would have to leave early, and wondering why I had agreed to give up two days for a sabbath retreat when I had so much to accomplish that week.

When I got about two feet from Doreen, I abruptly stopped and noticed the drastic difference between her and me. I couldn't even tell you now what she looks like because the difference was not in our appearance but in the air around us. Standing in her presence I felt stillness. A calmness and peace emanated from her like nothing I had ever encountered—or even thought I could detect in people. But I felt as though all my busy, scattered stress collided with her quietude. I had no choice but to stop, slow down, and appreciate this moment of introduction and welcome stillness.

I found out through the course of the retreat that Doreen is a part-time hermit. She works as a therapist and spiritual director, but her daily life also includes three to five hours of silence and meditation—time for prayer, for walking, for listening to the birds, for scripture, and for painting icons. During the retreat, I found that Doreen listened not only to our words but also to our spirits. She talked to us from a place of peace and centeredness that I have only read about in the lives of the saints.

I realized that we do not have to choose between a contemplative life *or* a secular life. I began to see that rest and sabbath are not to be set apart from our daily living—after deadlines have passed or after a career or after children have grown. There are persons walking among us, like Doreen, who have created the space and discipline in their daily lives to *be* instead of *do* all the time. And all that time of *being* makes the *doing* much more focused, effective, and rich.

TOO BUSY TO HEAR GOD

Day 2 Exercise

READ 1 THESSALONIANS 5:15-19.

REFLECT Paul here urges early Christians to take up several practices important for living God's call, including to "pray without ceasing" (see verse 17).

Pay attention this week to the busyness of your days. Even when you feel distracted, you can pray without ceasing by saying a breath prayer to calm yourself and come back into the moment. Remember how to find your breath prayer:

First, choose the name of God that is most meaningful to you, for example, Friend, Comforter, Holy One.

Second, choose a phrase that expresses your deepest desire: "help me to be still" or "be present with me now." The entire prayer should be no more than six to eight syllables.

PRAY Practice your prayer now; say it easily as you breathe in and out.

ACT As you go about your day, keep your prayer going inside your mind and heart. Notice how it affects your attitude.

Day 2 Reading

Imagine Martha's entry in her journal after the events recorded in Luke 10:38-42: "The Lord answered her, 'Martha, Martha, you are worried and distracted by many things; there is need of only one thing.'"

Dear Diary,

I did it again. I got frustrated with Mary and yelled at her, in front of Jesus, of all people. But really, I was the one who made the meal, made sure everyone had a place to sit, got the candles out, served the food. It's always the same. I get everything ready, while Mary sits with the men, listening to their conversations. Then she gets to ask the questions and hear their stories. It's only later as I clean up that I hear about the events in my own house, secondhand.

Today when I snapped, Jesus told me I was getting worked up for nothing. He wasn't scolding me or yelling at me. He was inviting me to stop and join them. And so I sat, and listened—and I have never enjoyed an evening so much.

Jesus points out to Martha that she is too *busy*. It is interesting to note that the Chinese word for "busy" is composed of two characters: "heart" and "killing." Have you ever been so busy, like Martha, that you felt you were killing your heart?

We can lose perspective on why we are doing what we're doing. Then we cannot appreciate the place we are in, the people we are with, or the experience itself because of the drive to accomplish, to perfect, and to succeed. Jesus calls us to sit, listen, and appreciate each and every moment as a gift.

A RULE OF LIFE

Day 3 Exercise

READ HEBREWS 10:24-25.

REFLECT The author of Hebrews sees "meeting together" as an essential ingredient in the recipe for remaining true to your calling. "Meeting together" promotes listening for God and keeping the fire of God's love alive.

What would you list as ingredients in the recipe for staying in touch with and living by God's call? Draw a Recipe for Life card. Start by naming your deepest hungers and desires for your life. Next, write what you believe your purpose is at this point in your life. Finally, list the ingredients and directions that will help you fulfill your desires and faithfully live out your purpose in life.

Your ingredients might include commitments like these: regular exercise, fifteen to twenty minutes of silence each day, calling your grandmother once a week, performing an act of kindness for someone every day, attending worship regularly, meeting with a spiritual mentor once a month, singing or listening to spiritual music, and so forth. Write your own recipe, or "rule of life," in your journal. Select just three or four commitments you consider essential.

PRAY Offer your recipe to God. Listen for what God would add or subtract. What is most important? What might you have left out?

ACT As a start, live out one commitment from your recipe. Notice how one consistent change can transform your life in ways you never imagined.

Day 3 Reading

There are several things in my life I cannot live without—air, water, shelter, family, and Girls' Night Out (GNO). Over the past four years GNO has become as essential to my mental and spiritual health as the basic elements of life. I have committed with six other women to meet every Tuesday night for good food, conversation, and accountability. We celebrate new relationships and graduations. We console one another in sickness and grief. We talk about family and politics and movies. We laugh! And we try to help each other live healthy lives of integrity, balance, and joy.

I will turn down parties, other gatherings, and dinner invitations to protect my Tuesday nights. I could not even tell you what TV shows are on Tuesday nights. Some people look at me a little strangely when I turn them down for what may seem a frivolous, estrogen-filled evening. Others get frustrated when I let this one commitment dictate my calendar. But this small group is vital to my spiritual formation.

When a friend and I started meeting four years ago on Tuesday nights, I had no idea that one commitment could so transform my perspective on life, broaden my thinking horizons, deepen my faith, and teach me the meaning of true friendship. These women help me live out my beliefs and intentions more faithfully.

If I were to develop a personal rule of life—a document to record my spiritual aim in life, as well as specific practices for suggesting that aim—Girls' Night Out would be one of the first rules of my life. This one commitment has become a covenant not only with the women with whom I meet but also with my family and friends who recognize that I'm a more healthy, centered, and enjoyable person to be around when I go to GNO every Tuesday.

Listen for what belongs in your rule. A rule of life enables us to listen consistently to God.

LISTENING TO THE WORLD

Day 4 Exercise

READ MICAH 6:8.

REFLECT Micah conveniently summarizes the way of life to which God calls us: "to do justice, and to love kindness, and to walk humbly with your God."

Make three columns in your journal, one for each aspect of living by God's call: do justice, love kindness, and walk humbly with your God. Before you pray today, take time to read or watch the news (you might try a website like www.CNN.com or the British Broadcasting Corporation, http://www.bbc.co.uk/). Ask yourself where you hear God's call to justice, kindness, or humility. Write what you hear under the appropriate columns.

PRAY Pray for those who desire justice, need healing, are being persecuted, or long for compassion.

ACT Sign up for a weekly e-mail from World in Prayer by subscribing at www.worldinprayer.org.

Day 4 Reading

In our church youth group there is one young man who reads the local
newspaper every morning, reads *National Geographic Magazine* every
month, and reads history books in his spare time. I learned this about Tim
at Bible study on Wednesday nights. During scripture study or when we
shared joys and concerns, Tim would offer an illustration or insight from
the world around us: local policy decisions, a natural disaster, or an
international event. I was impressed with his reading commitment and
ability to remember so much information. More importantly, I learned
from Tim the value of being aware of the world around me in relation to
my faith.

Being a disciple of Jesus means listening to the cries, needs, and groans
of all God's children and all God's creation. Jesus' disciples span the globe
and live in circumstances both similar to mine and so different that only in
my imagination can I envision their lives.

It is naive to pray only for the joys and concerns of our congregation
when people in our own city are losing their health care because of
government cutbacks and whole nations are in the midst of war. It is
impossible for me to reduce damage to the environment if I do not take
time to learn how my own actions contribute to wasting our precious
resources.

Tim taught me that I cannot read, study, and pray in a vacuum. Part of
living out my calling requires awareness of the world, the people, and the
environment around me. This effort takes time, and I have to be intentional
about it. But when I tune in to the joys and trials beyond my own
immediate circle, I have found my prayer life to be more meaningful, and I
see more clearly God's incredible love and compassion for all of creation. I
feel called to be more sensitive, compassionate, and active in the world and
realize tangible ways to help bring about the kingdom of God on earth.

Day 5 Exercise

READ 1 CORINTHIANS 12:14-27.

REFLECT Living by God's call means listening for God's call and gifts in others as well as in yourself, and that requires the kind of humility we see in Jesus.

As you read 1 Corinthians 12:14-27, listen for how you fit into the body of Christ. Are you the visible, active hands and feet of Christ in the world? Or are you a less noticeable but vital part of the body? Pray that God will reveal how you function in the community of Christ.

PRAY Make a list of others in your group. Bring each person to mind in a prayerful way. Listen for the gift(s) that each one has brought to the group. Write the gift(s) next to each individual's name in your journal.

ACT Tell someone today the gift she or he embodies or brings to a situation.

Day 5 Reading

A profoundly significant part of our calling as Jesus' disciples is willingness to serve others. We see Jesus throughout his life humbling himself to socialize with and serve the very people society instructed him to avoid. Learning humility may be one of the toughest lessons of our lives because our own society measures us by the honors we accumulate. Scripture offers us a radically alternative view.

In 1 Corinthians 12:14-27 we are reminded that we should regard no person more highly than another or make judgments based on our differences. Instead, we are to recognize our dependence on one another and celebrate all that we can accomplish together as opposed to competing with one another. *The Upper Room Dictionary of Christian Spiritual Formation* states, "At its core, true humility means recognizing that God has created us out of nothing and that God has given us all our abilities, aptitudes, and accomplishments as gifts of grace."[2]

As one who has always struggled with pride, I did not understand the true meaning of humility until I went on a high-ropes course with my junior high youth group. We were given the task of climbing a forty-foot rope ladder with a partner. Being athletic and strong myself, I graciously accepted a sixth-grade, rail-thin girl as my partner. But I discovered by the second of seven rungs that she was the one who had been gracious. Marie Claire could easily jump from one rung to the next, while I struggled, huffed and puffed, and got nowhere. We did end up reaching the top, but it was I who had to stand on her bent leg in order to jump and haul myself to the next rung.

The *Dictionary* goes on to say, "Our true uniqueness arises only out of our ability to respond to God's call for us—to nurture the gifts God has given us so as to become who God calls us to be."

That day I would have been more gratified to haul Marie Claire up the ladder, but we both learned more about our unique callings and gifts by nurturing each other and achieving *together* the task before us.

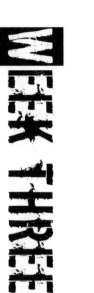

In order to answer God's call on our continuing journey, we need to know ourselves. We need to know who we really are—called by name and beloved. We also need to know that God places gifts in each pilgrim's satchel. This week we will explore and name those gifts. Plan now to spend some time on the gifts inventory found on pages 72–77 of this book or online at www.elca.org/youth/resource/inventory.html.

GROWING IN OUR GIFTS

Day 1 Exercise

READ EPHESIANS 4:7-13.

REFLECT God does not send us out into the world without equipping us for the ministry to which we are called. Nor does God send us out alone. God equips each of us with "gifts" to contribute to "building up the body of Christ" and for maturing in "the full stature of Christ."

Meditate on how you and your *Way of Pilgrimage* group have matured spiritually. What gifts do you need in order to mature "to the measure of the full stature of Christ"? Imagine what such maturity would look like for each person in your group.

PRAY Pray for each group member to mature in using the gifts God has given him or her.

ACT Begin the spiritual gifts inventory that starts on page 72 or go online at http://www.elca.org/youth/resource/inventory.html.

Day 1 Reading

When my sister and I were growing up, my sister was recognized as the social child, and I was labeled the academic child. My sister had many friends, went out every weekend, talked a lot on the phone, did the bare minimum for school, and freely expressed her emotions. I on the other hand had a few close friends, was usually home by 9:00 p.m., happily read novels, did my homework, and lived life on an even emotional keel. We grew up living contentedly with these labels and identities.

When we went to college, my sister realized she is a great student, capable of good grades and academic accomplishment. And I, in turn, found that people came to me with their problems, trusting me with joys and troubles. Still, our childhood labels were powerful shapers of our sense of identity.

Only in the past few years have my sister and I begun to realize how those labels limited what we tried and could accomplish. Boxing ourselves into such a small definition of self meant it took a long time to discover some of our God-given gifts. When my sister went to work for a well-known tutoring organization for students, she realized that she is a gifted teacher. And now that she has been promoted to manager with many administrative duties, she finds herself more organized and capable than her "high school self" would have been given credit for. On the flip side, as I followed my call into ministry, I discovered a great capacity for passion, compassion, and empathy for persons experiencing grief, pain, and joy. Not what you would expect from the placid bookworm of high school.

We each have a multitude of gifts. Some are close to the surface and easy to identify; others require us to stretch and try new things in order to discover the depth and beauty of who God has created us to be.

DISCOVER NEW GIFTS

Day 2 Exercise

READ 1 CORINTHIANS 12:4-27.

REFLECT God gives each of us a "manifestation of the Spirit for the common good," gifts for contributing to the ministry of Christ's body in the world. Meditate on the mystery of your relationship with Christ and your dependence on all believers for building up the full ministry of Christ. No one has all the gifts that are needed! Not even one congregation or denomination can claim all the gifts.

Draw an image of a physical body. Think of this as the body of Christ represented by your group or congregation. Figuratively speaking, where would you locate yourself and your gifts on this body? Name the gifts implied by your location.

PRAY Hold each member of your group in prayer. Let the Spirit help you to recognize what part of the body of Christ each of them best represents, and draw the individuals onto your symbolic picture.

ACT Prepare to affirm the gifts you see in the others in your upcoming group meeting. Also, if you have not done it yet, complete the spiritual gifts inventory on pages 72–77 or online at http://www.elca.org/youth/resource/inventory.html.

Day 2 Reading

God knit you together in your mother's womb and knows you intimately. God knows not only your flaws and failures but more importantly each of your gifts and all that you are capable of. God has given you gifts to be used, developed, and offered for the glory of God. Just as with people of faith throughout history, God has already called you to be who you are uniquely in the world.

In scripture God often calls people in unexpected ways that enable them to discover gifts they didn't know they had. When God called Moses to go back to Egypt and free the Israelites from Pharaoh's bondage, Moses resisted. He didn't think he was the right man for the job. But God saw gifts in Moses he couldn't see in himself.

When Jesus called Simon and Andrew to leave their fishing nets and follow him, they did so immediately, raising no objections. But they had no idea what was in store for them. If they'd had a clue what following Jesus would actually mean, they probably would have said, "We're simple fishermen. We don't have what it takes for this kind of life!"

The callings of Moses and Jesus' disciples were as different as night and day. Each of us will also receive our calling in individual ways: some will be consistent messages over the course of a lifetime; others will be like lightning bolts from the sky. Some of us may hear a calling directly from God through prayer and meditation. Others may be called through the invitation of a pastor or the voice of a friend. The challenge for each of us is to be open to the calling and ready to say yes. It is in following the call that we discover the truth of our gifts, as God's Spirit empowers us to discover, develop, and use them.

FEAR OF USING OUR GIFTS

Day 3 Exercise

READ MATTHEW 25:14-30.

REFLECT Meditate on the good news reflected in this parable: God has given gifts to each of us for the increase of God's kingdom on earth.

Reflect on the kinds of servants Jesus describes in the parable of the talents. In what ways do you see yourself in these characters?

PRAY Name your fear of using your gifts. Pray that each member of your group may discover his or her gifts and use them well rather than bury, hide, or withhold them.

ACT Complete the spiritual gifts inventory on pages 72–77 or go online at http://www.elca.org/youth/resource/inventory.html. If you have completed your inventory, score it. If you have scored your inventory, try to live today in the awareness of the unique gifts God has given you to share.

Day 3 Reading

It is an understatement to call my friend Susanna an overachiever. She always reads everything assigned to her, never misses a deadline, writes first and second drafts of papers, and becomes the leader of any organization she joins. Do you know people like this? The beautiful thing about Susanna is that she is also kind, compassionate, and extremely funny—someone you want to be around. And that is what got her in trouble recently.

The class assignment was to pair up with one other person to research and write a twenty-page paper. The first person to approach Susanna about sharing the assignment was a procrastinator and a poor writer. But she told Susanna how much she appreciated her ideas and said how much she would enjoy working with Susanna. Against her better judgment, Susanna consented to be her partner. Can you guess who read all the resources, did most of the research, and rewrote a great deal of the paper?

Susanna's project partner was not lacking in gifts. She had a wonderful imagination, fine artistic ability, and a real heart for people in trouble. But she lacked confidence in herself and didn't see these gifts as valuable, especially in academics. So she tended to bury her talents.

Recognizing our own gifts and limitations takes a great deal of life experience and maturity. We can accept the affirmation and encouragement of people we trust to clarify our gifts. We can be willing to try new things that allow us to discover gifts and grow our talents. We need to be humble enough to admit that we don't possess *all* gifts and we have much to learn from others. And we need to be gracious enough to offer our gifts in order to build up those around us.

Ministry is always a partnership in which everyone exercises the gifts they have, and no one withholds what he or she has to offer. If we are to be the body of Christ, we must call forth and affirm each and every member's gifts. When God gives us gifts, we are responsible to use them to the fullest of our ability.

USING GIFTS TO SHARE GOD'S LOVE

Day 4 Exercise

READ 1 CORINTHIANS 12:31–13:13.

REFLECT God gives us not only the gifts (physical and mental equipment, ability, know-how) to live out our calling but the love to do it without self at the center, for the sake of others in Christ's name.

Meditate on the nature of "the greater gifts" of love described by Paul. Consider the spirit in which you have done your work, participated in activities, or helped others during the past week. When have you done so grudgingly and when in "the more excellent way"?

Down one side of a journal page make a list of all the qualities of love Paul names in 1 Cor. 13:4-7. On the other side of the page make a list of your group's members, including yourself. Draw connections between love qualities and names, identifying where you see the love of Christ active in and among you.

PRAY Open your heart to the gift of God's love poured out on us through Christ. Open your heart to pour out that love for others today.

ACT With each and every encounter today, let the gift of God's love be outpoured through you.

Day 4 Reading

Writing in *Wishful Thinking: A Seeker's ABC*, Frederick Buechner helps us understand the connection between our calling and our gifts. The passion between lovers, the sympathy among friends, or the radical love of forgiveness, all these are forms of love. Each entails an ability to lose oneself—in another's arms, in another's company, or in the suffering of others—and therefore find love as God desires it. "Love," Buechner says, "is not primarily an emotion, but an act of the will. When Jesus tells us to love our neighbors, he is not telling us to love them in the sense of responding to them with a cozy emotional feeling. You can as easily produce a cozy emotional feeling on demand as you can a yawn or a sneeze."[1]

Instead, Jesus wants us to *choose* to love our neighbors enough to work for their well-being, even if it requires making sacrifices along the way. When we choose to love our neighbors, we may be surprised to find that we can serve those around us without even liking them very much.

Our calling asks us to love people in the messiness of life. Whether someone needs a ride, needs to talk late into the night, or needs to hear he or she is making unhealthy decisions, God calls us not only to help but to do so with an attitude of love.

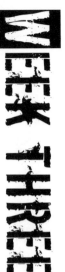
BEING CHRIST TO OTHERS

Day 5 Exercise

READ MARK 7:31-37.

REFLECT Mark's Gospel (7:31-37) tells the story of Jesus healing a deaf man. Jesus took the man away from the crowds, healed him, and then instructed him to tell no one about the miracle.

Some of us enjoy public displays of kindness and generosity. Others prefer to work behind the scenes and not receive credit for the good work we do. Ponder the advantages and disadvantages of each approach. Which approach are you more drawn to? Write why in your journal.

PRAY Pray for grace to be like Jesus with the deaf man in this story from Mark. Ask God to help you be Christ to others without seeking recognition or affirmation.

ACT Find a way in the next twenty-four hours to give someone a gift anonymously. Is your gift appreciated? Do you even know? Do you feel the same satisfaction as when a person knows you were the source of assistance?

Day 5 Reading

A youth group found an incredible way to practice and witness the effect of grace in people's lives. The group spent six weeks studying the Bible and learning about grace. Then the youth leader and volunteers asked each member of the group to bring five dollars to church one Tuesday night. They collected the money and took it to a diner down the street. There the leader and the restaurant manager agreed that the money would be used to pay the bill anonymously for seven tables of diners that evening.

The youth began arriving at the diner in groups of two, three, or four and took seats at different tables. None of the customers noticed that an entire youth group was present, waiting and watching to see how people would react to their offerings of grace. The youth did not have to wait long.

Four elderly women eating dinner at one table had been rather glum and quiet, talking intermittently and sometimes snapping at one another. When it came time to pay, their waitress informed them that their bill had already been paid. The transformation was immediate. They became more animated, smiling and giggling as they asked who had been so kind. The waitress said she could not tell them but encouraged them to enjoy their evening. They left arm-in-arm with smiles on their faces, looking younger than when they had come in.

Across the diner, the reaction was totally different. A middle-aged man and woman asked their waiter repeatedly to tell them who had paid for their meal. When the waiter refused, insisting that this was a gift, the couple became more and more agitated and even angry. They wanted to know who had paid for the meal or to pay it for themselves. They left confused and breathing heavily.

One man, when told that his meal was covered, took out more than double what his meal had cost. He gave it to the waitress and asked her to use it to cover another couple's meal without telling them who had paid. Grace often begets more grace.

When we risk being Christ to others, we must be prepared, as Jesus was, for delight and gratitude, doubt and rejection, or responsive generosity. Regardless of outcome, Jesus calls us to live out the same grace that he lived.

As we continue our pilgrimage, we begin to seek our specific pathway—the plan, the journey, the individual path God has for each of us. Seeking this distinctive path means discerning our vocation. The word *vocation* comes from the Latin word *vocare*, which means "to call." When we talk about personal vocation, we don't necessarily mean final career plans or church-based ministry. Our call in life may be expressed through several career changes, though larger trends will usually become apparent along the way. Use your journal this week to note trends and yearnings you are aware of at this stage in your life.

THE WORK TO WHICH YOU ARE CALLED

Day 1 Exercise

Frederick Buechner writes that vocation is "where your deep gladness and the world's deep hunger meet."[1] Your vocation may be clearly revealed to you early in life, or you may spend years exploring different careers and volunteer activities before you discern your true calling.

REFLECT Explore your vocation by making two lists in your journal:

1. What gives you the greatest joy, energy, and peace?
2. What place, people, or situation in the world concerns you deeply and draws your deepest compassion?

Do you see ways in which your deep gladness may intersect with the world's deep need? Draw the intersection in you, labeling the lines.

PRAY Write a prayer expressing how you see these areas intersecting or how you would like to see them joined.

ACT Choose one way today to find out more about either your deep gladness or your deep concern (more reflection, a conversation with someone you trust, Internet research).

Day 1 Reading

Over the past several weeks we have reflected on our own story, the presence of God in our life, and our personal gifts. We know God calls us in each moment to live lives of love and faithfulness—in our daily actions and interactions, even in the smallest decisions. But for what purpose? To *what* is God calling us? And where? And why? These are questions of vocation, the work a person is called to by God.

It seems that as soon as we enter kindergarten, people start asking, "What do you want to be when you grow up?" And that question continues all the way through high school. If we choose to attend college, the question becomes, "What will you major in?" As we get closer to graduation (from high school or college), people want to know, "Where are you going to work?" Even after we start working, we are asked, "What makes you happy?" or "If you could do anything in the world, what would it be?"

The question of vocation is bigger, deeper, and more profound than any of these questions. Some might say that it is simpler too. Maybe kindergartners answer the question of vocation most clearly, because children usually choose to do what makes them happy. Their ideas of what to be are not yet clouded by salary ranges or social prestige. And they know the value of helping others.

God calls us to work that brings us joy and meets the needs of the world. We are truly blessed when we pour ourselves into service because of the joy that it brings. When our gifts, joy, satisfaction, and peace combine in our work, then we can be confident of a vocation found!

YOUR SERVANT IS LISTENING

Day 2 Exercise

READ 1 SAMUEL 3:9-10.

REFLECT Eli helped Samuel learn to listen and to recognize God's voice (as we saw in Volume 4), and in doing so, he helped Samuel discover his vocation in life.

Who are the "Elis" in your life, people who have encouraged you and pointed to God's work in your life? How have they facilitated your listening to God or recognizing your gifts?

PRAY Ask God for guidance, and spend time listening for God's call to you. Repeat Samuel's plea, "Speak, for your servant is listening" (1 Sam. 3:10). Keep in mind your deep gladness and the world's need as you wait for guidance.

ACT Do you know a few people who don't recognize the gifts that God has given them to help others? Find a way to be an Eli and tell them.

Day 2 Reading

I spent the first two years of divinity school telling everyone how sure I was that I would not go into vocational ministry. I had a convincing list of reasons, including my greater interest in academics than ministry. Plus, I did not have the compassion and empathy necessary for pastoral ministry.

Looking back, I had heard the call of God several times in the night, but, like Samuel, did not recognize God's voice. I did enjoy study, but I really loved teaching the older adult Sunday school class at my church, hearing their stories, and learning to love them. I did not cry at movies or readily share my feelings as easily as some, but my husband pointed out that the phone would ring every week with someone on the other end asking for advice or consolation. Although I resisted my pastor's invitation to preach during my time as an intern, I was surprised to find that I loved the preparation and the delivery of sermons and that my words touched people in the congregation.

Still, I said I was not called to ministry. But, like Samuel, I had "Eli" in my life, who pointed to God in the midst of my experience. My professors encouraged me to think beyond the limitations I had set for myself. My friends smiled and nodded knowingly as I recounted new experiences and "Aha!" moments. My pastor named gifts in me that I had been unable to see in myself.

In their own ways, these persons told me to go back to where I had heard the whisperings, to ask God for guidance, and to listen for all that God would reveal. This advice still holds true as I continue to discern my vocation.

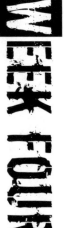
PREPARED TO LEAD BY FOLLOWING FIRST

Day 3 Exercise

READ 1 SAMUEL 3:9-10.

REFLECT Many influences prepared Samuel for his vocational path: a mother who prayed, the voice of God within him, an old mentor named Eli. Similarly, God uses many influences, large and small, to prepare us to follow and serve in ways we could never imagine. That's why we learn ways to pay attention.

Saint Ignatius (sixteenth century) sought a way to pray that would focus his awareness on God's presence in all that he did. It is called the prayer of examen. To use this prayer in its simplest form, we look back over the day in quiet reflection, asking two questions:

1. Where did I feel close to (or aware of) God?
2. Where did I feel separate from (or unaware of) God?

Take time to examine the last twenty-four hours with these two questions. Look for God moving in and through your life. Where is God opening doors for you in the midst of daily life? How are you responding?

PRAY Pray, "Speak, Lord, your servant is listening." Wherever you felt closest to God, listen for what God was saying. Wherever you felt furthest from God, listen for what was going on.

ACT In the midst of your day, practice awareness of the times and places you feel close or far from God. Pay attention to what, inside or outside yourself, is affecting your spiritual openness.

Day 3 Reading

Being the new person is never easy. Starting a new school or walking into a room where it's obvious everyone already knows one another can be torture. I felt the mixed dread and anticipation of being the new kid the first time I walked into the campus ministry house at college. It was a bring-a-friend-the-first-week-of-classes party. I hung back, just behind my friend, but I wasn't allowed to stay in my friend's shadow for long.

Tim, the campus minister, came striding over and grabbed my hand. I don't think he was taller than average, but it looked as if he'd borrowed a larger person's legs and head for the day. He seemed like a bobble-head on stilts coming at me with this goofy but heartwarming grin. Tim asked my name once and, despite the chaos that day, never had to ask me again. And he did the same with every person who walked into the house. He had the gift of memorizing names and faces immediately so that we always felt welcomed and special.

During my first three years at school I spent countless hours each week at that house—Sunday night fellowship, Wednesday night Bible study, Friday morning prayers, plus dropping by just to see who was there or ask Tim's advice on life, love, and the future. The seniors seemed to have everything under control, welcoming visitors, setting up tables and chairs, and answering all our questions with insight and intelligence. But at the end of my junior year, Tim called a few of us aside and pointed out that the next year we would need to step up and become the leaders the seniors had been for us. It had never occurred to me that I would be asked to serve or that I had the ability to do so. But the next fall I got my chance, and I found that the example had been set before me by Tim and the other leaders.

I began to understand that if we pay attention and soak life in, then when we are called to give back, we will have the ability, confidence, and desire to do for others as others have done for us.

ANSWERING GOD'S CALL WITH A LOAF OF BREAD

Day 4 Exercise

READ JOHN 6:5-13.

REFLECT Discovering our vocation is like the little boy realizing the Lord needs exactly what he has to give on any given day, even gifts as simple as a few loaves and fishes.

On a sheet of paper write down the hours of the day from the time you get up to the time you go to bed. Then fill in your activities from the day before. Circle those times you felt able to offer your gifts when God needed them. Put an arrow next to those times you had gifts to offer but chose not to do so or didn't recognize the opportunity.

PRAY In the spirit of the little boy in the story, offer Jesus the gift of your life—all you have and all you are—for today. Ask him to show you today where he needs you.

ACT Take a penny from your pocket or wallet. Place it on a table and leave it as a token of your willingness to give of yourself today.

Day 4 Reading

Too often we get overwhelmed when we begin to think about our *vocation.* People think that finding their vocation means finding the perfect career or impacting the world in a huge and newsworthy way or finding an inner peace that radiates a golden glow. When we set our standards that high, it is easy to become overcome with frustration or to believe that God has not called us in any specific or unique way. But consider the familiar story of the boy with the loaves and the fishes:

> When he looked up and saw a large crowd coming toward him, Jesus said to Philip, "Where are we to buy bread for these people to eat?" He said this to test him, for he himself knew what he was going to do. Philip answered him, "Six months' wages would not buy enough bread for each of them to get a little." One of his disciples, Andrew, Simon Peter's brother, said to him, "There is a boy here who has five barley loaves and two fish. But what are they among so many people?" Jesus said, "Make the people sit down." Now there was a great deal of grass in the place; so they sat down, about five thousand in all. Then Jesus took the loaves, and when he had given thanks, he distributed them to those who were seated; so also the fish, as much as they wanted. When they were satisfied, he told his disciples, "Gather up the fragments left over, so that nothing may be lost." So they gathered them up, and from the fragments of the five barley loaves, left by those who had eaten, they filled twelve baskets.—John 6:5-13

Did this boy find his vocation? Yes! He did not have to become a missionary in a faraway land or work in a church. Some may find their vocation in those situations, but most of us will find our calling in the everyday occurrences of our lives.

Our calling does not have to be "religious"; it does not even have to be a career. Our vocation as followers of Jesus is choosing to make decisions in everyday life—as a teacher, a parent, a stockbroker, or a plumber—that honor God and serve the least among us.

PRACTICING THE PRESENCE OF GOD

Day 5 Exercise

READ LUKE 10:25-28.

"You shall love the Lord your God with all your heart, and with all your soul, and with all your strength, and with all your mind. . . ."
—Luke 10:27

REFLECT Whether your vocation right now is to knit sweaters, go to school, mow lawns, or feed the hungry in Christ's name, it can become a way to love God with all your being and love your neighbor as yourself—our primary calling as people of God. Vocation is a way to practice the presence of God in our lives.

What activity do you already do every day that reminds you of God's presence? It may be walking to class, practicing dance, or tutoring after school.

PRAY Ask Jesus, "What must I do to inherit the life God wants to give me?" Listen for his answer.

ACT Choose a daily activity that will serve as a cue for remembering God's love and turning the moment into an occasion for loving.

Day 5 Reading

My husband told me that he has found the perfect opening line for his first novel: "My wife starting knitting last week . . ." He found it so amusing when I started knitting. As I learned this new craft, I would sit for hours knitting long strips out of scrap yarn my mother-in-law had given me. Eventually I bought yarn and graduated to full scarves. By the time Christmas came, I gave four scarves and even a hat as gifts! My husband was baffled by all this time sitting with yarn and needles. In his imaginary novel he made up motivations for my new hobby ranging from the onset of deep depression to a mysterious transformation from raging feminist to house frau.

In reality the motivation was much more mundane. Knitting relaxed me. When I sat down with the yarn I could be tired or stressed or frustrated, but as the scarf began to lengthen on my lap I could feel my shoulders relax, my breathing become more even, and my mind begin to clear. It was as effective as any prayer I had experimented with. As an added bonus, I had something to show for my time and effort—something others could wear to be reminded of my love and care for them.

My mother-in-law—and knitting teacher—showed me a book last week that confirmed my gut reaction to the benefits of knitting. It's called *Knitting into the Mystery: A Guide to the Shawl-Knitting Ministry*. It tells how two women began a ministry in their church of knitting shawls for persons who needed an extra bit of love: new moms and new babies, individuals in hospice care, and widows. The two women pray as they knit and give the gifts with a printed prayer.

For me, knitting has become a way to practice the presence of God. It slows and quiets the mind long enough to listen for God to speak. Jesus did not command the disciples to knit. But I know the great fathers and mothers of the desert often wove baskets out of marsh reeds as they prayed. Perhaps I have discovered one of their secrets! For the simple rhythmic motion of knitting brings me as close to God as silence or daily prayer.

As we journey on, we find that the more present we are to God, the more present we are to ourselves and those around us. The call of the pilgrim is to be available to God and to fellow travelers. This week we will explore how the quality of our response to God's call may depend more on how Christ works in and through our weakness than on how much we can do for Christ through our strengths. The way of the cross invites us to see that God sometimes works more powerfully in and through our weakness. Keep your journals handy for these reflections.

THE STORY OF GOD IN YOUR LIFE

Day 1 Exercise

READ 2 CORINTHIANS 4:5-7.

REFLECT To live by God's call means making ourselves available to the power of the Spirit within us. When we become available to the Spirit, our personal stories become part of God's great story of redeeming love, despite our weaknesses. Paul described it as having "treasure in clay jars."

Go find a jar or cup and hold it. Think of it as a symbol of your life. In your journal, jot down thoughts about these questions:

- Where did your life come from; whose hands helped make and mold it?
- What experiences have made it stronger or weaker?
- What is its purpose, and when does it prove particularly useful?
- When has it gotten cracked, and how it has been repaired?

PRAY Hold out your cup to God. What does God put in it? Who is it for?

ACT Carry this cup with you today as a reminder of your purpose and value as a fragile clay jar. If someone asks about it, say what God has put in your cup.

Day 1   Reading

They say that hindsight is 20/20. It's easy for us to look back and see God at work in the lives of Abraham and Sarah, Moses, Esther, Mary, and Jesus. As we read their stories from the vantage point of our own century, it's obvious to us that they had a clear calling in life. Even in more recent history most of us would say Dorothy Day and Martin Luther King Jr. had clear vocations they could not help but follow. We see their callings because we have the full story, from beginning to end. But what about our story? Where is God at work in our life?

Singer and songwriter Peter Mayer has written about this desire to know our own purpose, to see our story clearly written out. Mayer expresses frustration that he knows the stories of noble characters in Shakespeare's plays and the history of nations, but he cannot see clearly the story of his own life. The beauty of language used to describe gods in famous myths and princesses saved in fairy tales amazes him, but no gilded pages tell the story of his life.

Throughout the song, Mayer pleads, "Now can anybody, please tell me the story of my life?"[1] We all hope that our stories thus far are the beginning of a wonderful epic, a story in which faith and wisdom result in an admirable and productive life. We hope for a life more filled with blessings than crises. And we long for a happy ending.

But no one can know or tell us the complete story of our life. The best we can do is to write the story along with God. We can look back to see where God has been at work, where we find evidence of God's hand shaping and prompting. Once we begin to recognize God working in the past, it is easier to see God working in the present and to continue writing our story with God into the future.

CALLED TO CHANGE THE WORLD

Day 2 Exercise

READ 2 CORINTHIANS 4:7-12.

REFLECT To live by God's call means making ourselves available in any situation to Christ's love at work among people, even at the risk of getting criticized or discouraged by people's responses. Paul assures us that, in the midst of persecution, "the life of Jesus" within Christians shone through all the more. The same will be true for us.

When have you felt "afflicted . . . perplexed. . . persecuted. . . struck down" in the course of trying to be a faithful witness to Christ's love? What enables you to persevere so you are not "not crushed . . . not driven to despair . . . not forsaken . . . not destroyed?"

PRAY Share with God where your clay jar is at risk of cracking under the pressure outside you. Turn your attention to the positive pressure of Christ's Spirit within you at the point where you feel vulnerable to cracking. Feel the strength of the Spirit from within.

ACT When experiencing outside pressure, let the life of Jesus be strong within you. Imagine and do what he would if he were in your situation.

Day 2 Reading

Once we hear and begin to follow our calling in life, it may take us in unexpected directions and into frightening places. Our vocation may call us to end friendships or relationships; it may call us to move to a new place or to stand up to people in power. Living faithfully in this world often means making decisions that are confusing or seem foolish to those around us.

I recently read about a group of people who found themselves led to unexpected action. Students at Georgetown University learned that many workers on their campus did not earn a living wage. These workers' annual salaries could not provide the basic necessities of life: food, shelter, and health care. Many students recognized the injustice of the situation and founded the Living Wage Coalition to advocate for these workers and seek justice. When the Living Wage Coalition could not succeed in convincing the administration to raise wages for the campus employees, twenty-five students organized a hunger strike. They declared that they would not eat until the university administration agreed to raise the wages of the support staff.

Why would these college students deprive themselves of food for people they did not even know? Was a stranger's well-being worth jeopardizing their own health, giving up class and study time to demonstrate, and risking backlash from their own university? These twenty-five students believed so and were willing to make public choices to express their beliefs.

A striker explained, "One's belief in God and in the fundamental goodness and dignity of every person must be grounded in action and not just wishing for things to change." In the end, the university accepted the students' proposal for a wage increase and agreed to give employees the right to form unions so they can advocate for themselves.[2]

The call to follow Christ may be scary and involve personal risk at times, but when the Spirit calls us to change the world so it looks more like what God intended, how can we say no?

WEEK FIVE A PILGRIM'S VULNERABILITY AND AVAILABILITY

GOD'S PERSISTENCE

Day 3 Exercise

READ 2 CORINTHIANS 4:7-12 AGAIN TODAY.

REFLECT Living by God's call is not about living your life as others would live it but as Jesus would if he were in your place. In Paul's words, it is letting the "the life of Jesus" live in you and shine through you when society or instinct would direct you otherwise.

Select one situation (family, school, work, friendship) that you are finding hard to deal with in a spirit of love and charity. In three columns, write your answers to these questions: (*a*) How would most people react in this situation? (*b*) What is my natural instinct? (*c*) How would Jesus respond if he were in my place?

PRAY Ask for God's blessing on the person, people, or situation that so challenges you. Pray for strength and grace to respond as you believe Jesus would in these circumstances.

ACT Do as you imagine Jesus would do if he were in your place.

Day 3 Reading

One of the most interesting times in divinity school is when students share the stories of their call. The ones who came to ministry as a second (or third) career especially intrigued me. As I listened to Steve's story, I heard how patient and persistent God can be in revealing a calling.

Steve grew up as a preacher's kid—not the wild and rebellious PK but a gifted, compassionate leader in the church from a young age. Yet when it came time to make decisions about where he would go to college and what he would major in, he did not choose a small liberal arts school or a major in philosophy and religion. No, Steve went to a big state school and majored in business. He remained faithful and committed to the church, but he believed his gifts, intelligence, and leadership abilities were meant for the business world.

And he became very successful. He landed great internships in college, graduated magna cum laude, and was able to choose from three different job offers right after graduation. He took the job back in his hometown and kept his commitment to his local church, serving on committees and helping with the youth group. He married a wonderful woman and was promoted at work. People began asking him when he would go into the ministry. But he assured them that since his career was going so well, he was where God wanted him.

When he began to have thoughts about ministry himself, he pushed them aside as long as he could. Then he made a deal with God, "First, I'll get my Masters in Business Administration (MBA). Then I'll apply to divinity school. But you'll see; I won't be accepted." Well, after he received his MBA, he was promoted at work *and* accepted into divinity school. So then he told God, "Well, okay, I'll go. But I'll keep my job too, because you must want me to be a minister with the people I work with. Surely you don't want me in the church full-time."

Even as I heard Steve tell his story during his final year of divinity school, he was serving a local church while retaining his marketing job.

God can call us through other people, through our own prayers and devotions, and through affirmation of our gifts. But we always have the choice to say yes or no to our call. God will be patient and use us wherever we are.

RADICAL OPENNESS TO THE SPIRIT OF GOD

Day 4 Exercise

READ 2 CORINTHIANS 4:7-12 AGAIN.

REFLECT Living by God's call is not about trying harder to be good on your own energy but living in the energy and influence of Christ's spirit within you, as an individual and in a group. Even when we are dying under the pressures of the world or the sacrifices we make for others, spiritually we survive and thrive by paying attention to the promptings of the Holy Spirit, what Paul calls "the life of Jesus" in us.

When have you had a sense of God repeatedly prompting you to remember someone, to do something, or to be careful about a course of action?

PRAY Open yourself to God's presence and prompting. What is God saying? Where is God leading?

ACT Cooperate with what the Spirit is urging you to do, even if you don't know why.

Day 4 Reading

I am in a Covenant Discipleship group. Five of us first met eight months ago to develop the covenant that would guide our personal and communal discipleship. We covenant to read scripture and pray for each other every day, to worship and receive Communion weekly, to participate in some form of outreach each month, and to speak out in the face of injustice. And our covenant ends with these two promises:

- I will obey the promptings of the Holy Spirit to serve God and my neighbor.
- I will heed the warnings of the Holy Spirit not to sin against God and my neighbor.[3]

These clauses remind us that our lives of faith are not a set of rules or a checklist of duties but a fluid and dynamic relationship with God. When one member received a Sunday-morning call from a friend in crisis, the prompting to be a friend was more important than attending church that morning. When a relative made a racist joke at Thanksgiving, the prompting was to speak to that person privately instead of creating a scene at the dinner table. God does not call us to lives dictated by rigid rules and expectations but to follow the Spirit's promptings of love, compassion, and justice.

Theologian Dorothee Soelle writes that the unique characteristic of Jesus was his radical availability to God's Spirit. She believes there was no boundary between God and Jesus; that Jesus was able to remove the ego, doubt, and selfishness that often serve as barriers to the Holy Spirit. In each moment, Jesus could discern and follow the promptings of the Holy Spirit. Thus he provided a model for his disciples of every age.

I have yet to experience such radical openness in my own spirit, but I have seen it in others; and I come together with fellow believers each week to remind myself of my commitments and my desire. I come to hear their stories, to learn from their experiences, and to share mine when it is appropriate. Discerning a call, whether in each moment or in a lifelong vocation, requires intention, self-discipline, community, and a radical openness to the Spirit of God.

WEEK FIVE A PILGRIM'S VULNERABILITY AND AVAILABILITY

YOUNG PEOPLE WHO LEAD BY EXAMPLE

Day 5 Exercise

READ 2 CORINTHIANS 4:7-12 AGAIN.

REFLECT To a society like ours that celebrates self-centeredness and individual glory Paul speaks joyfully of being available to live for the sake of others: "So death is at work in us, but life in you."

In his book *The Sacred Journey*, Frederick Buechner writes:

> To journey for the sake of having our own lives is little by little to cease to live in any sense that really matters, even to ourselves, because it is only by journeying for the world's sake—even when the world bores and sickens and scares you half to death—that little by little we start to come alive.[4]

Draw a horizontal line on a page in your journal. On one end, write "unavailable"; on the other end, write "entirely available." Mark where you feel you are on the continuum at this point in your life. What situations or practices help you be more available to God?

PRAY Ask God, "For whom do I live beyond myself? For whose sake am I here besides my own?" Write what comes to mind. Pray for greater desire to be available to the Spirit of power and grace.

ACT Choose one small pleasure to sacrifice today as a sign of your willingness to be more available to God for the sake of others.

Day 5 Reading

Have you ever found yourself in awe of someone? Have you ever wondered how someone could possess so much knowledge? act with such kindness all the time? be so athletic? be so wise and faithful in all circumstances?

I have been in awe of a certain young man since he was only sixteen years old. I first met him when he became chairperson of a denominational organization for which I worked. At sixteen he was funny, intelligent, prayerful, and a natural leader. I have been privileged to become and remain his friend over the past seven years. In that time I have seen him become chairperson of at least two other denominational organizations, wrestle with his own calling and career, speak truth and justice to persons in power, and be interviewed by reporters and even *TeenPeople*.

Jay has been able to see clearly where God is calling him and follow faithfully. The most unique chapters of his life are the two trips he has made to Sudan in an effort to document and expose the slavery that still exists there. God placed this cause and passion on Jay's heart in a most unusual way. Jay grudgingly went to a gospel concert with friends; during the concert he heard the startling facts and stories of families being separated; of men, women, and children being sold into slavery. He was shocked and appalled to hear that such atrocities could be allowed to continue even today. Being the person of faith and action I know him to be, he had made contact with a local organization trying to stop the slave trade and then decided to travel with them to Sudan. Risking his safety and possibly his freedom, Jay recorded interviews with women and children as they told their harrowing accounts of separation, abuse, and terror.

Jay's faithfulness is inspiring when you consider the risks and challenges he has been willing to undertake. But I am in awe of him most of all because he seeks to be as faithful in the daily decisions of his life as in the larger, life-changing moments.

WEEK FIVE A PILGRIM'S VULNERABILITY AND AVAILABILITY

So what does life look like now as we near the end of this stretch of pilgrimage? The beauty of pilgrimage is that it never ends. A flight back from one journey simply begins yet another journey. We are a pilgrim people, all trying to get back home to God. The question is whether we answer the call to continue to be pilgrims—being present to ourselves, our companions, those we meet along the way, and to the God of our journeys. Commit yourself anew to daily exercises this week and to a continued pilgrimage of faith in the weeks and months to come.

LIVING WITH HOPE

Day 1 Exercise

READ PSALM 103:1-5.

REFLECT Living God's call depends on our ability to trust God's grace, apart from which we lose faith and hope. Meditate on God's nature as expressed in this psalm. What affirmations of God's grace would you like to add from your own life?

Make a list of verbs in verses 3-5. Which of these touch your spirit and resonate most deeply with the work and call of God in you? Reflect on how they speak to you about your vocation from God.

PRAY Pray with the psalm verses that especially draw you, blessing God's holy name with all that is in you. Receive and rest in the blessing of God's peace.

ACT Do not forget God's benefits today. Share the grace with someone else.

Day 1 Reading

In a class on United Methodist theology we got into a conversation on economics and politics. I quickly became discouraged as I realized that many necessities of life have become privileges instead of rights in our society. We have public education, but wealthier neighborhoods have better public schools, and the wealthy have the option of sending their children to private schools while public schools suffer. We have amazing medical technology, but more and more people lack insurance and access to basic health care. Although many people have homes with a bedroom for every person in the family, others live on the streets.

I expressed my pessimistic view that we, as a society, would never rise above this state, that our human greed and ignorance would maintain the status quo. My professor quickly stopped me. "We are Christians," he said. "And therefore, by definition, we are people of hope. We live with a belief that God's kingdom will come on earth and that the poor, the widow, and the orphan will have all they need." He reminded me that hope should define my worldview. New life is always possible because Jesus has conquered fear, evil, and death. We must live our lives as evidence that we believe in Jesus' resurrection.

Madeleine L'Engle writes about this hope:

> *Sunday:*
> Dear God, He has come, the Word has come again.
> There is no terror left in silence, in clouds, in gloom.
> He has conquered the hate; he has overcome the pain.
> Where, days ago, was death lies only an empty tomb.
>
> The secret should have come to me with his birth,
> when glory shone through darkness, peace through strife.
> For every birth follows a kind of death,
> and only after pain comes life.[1]

Whether our vocation is crystal clear or a distant foggy vision, we must live confident of God's love for the world, as bearers of God's love to all the world. We may not see the hope and glory and possibilities in the various "births" of our lives, but if we live confident of God's desire and the power of divine love, then they will be revealed to us.

SENT OUT TO SERVE

Day 2 Exercise

READ ISAIAH 6:1-8.

If we trust God with our lives, we can risk responding to God's call. In Isaiah's vision, he experienced God both forgiving his past and calling him into the future. Isaiah's response, "Here am I," is an ancient expression of absolute trust and loving surrender to God.

REFLECT What past does God forgive and free you from ("your sin is blotted out," verse 7)? What future is God calling you into ("Whom shall I send…?" verse 8)? Reflect in your journal on these questions.

PRAY Sit with open hands and pray, "Here am I; send me." Offer yourself to be an answer to God's call in whatever form that may take.

ACT Live the spirit of the words, "Here am I; send me." Be available to God's prompting in all you do and say.

Day 2 Reading

Over the past two years I have found walking a labyrinth to be the most meaningful and illuminating time of prayer for me. Through the centuries, the labyrinth, an ancient tool for prayer and meditation, has been used to help people seeking discernment in their life's journey.

The labyrinth is a powerful symbol of spiritual journey introduced into medieval prayer practice when the traditional pilgrimages to the Holy Land became too dangerous for most travelers. In both that time and ours, people have found it fosters meditation. The labyrinth has only one path, so there are no dead ends. Each time one walks, the winding path provides different insights about life, relationships, and the journey with God.

There are three stages in walking a labyrinth: (1) *purgation*—as we enter the labyrinth we seek to let go of the details of life that keep us from God; (2) *illumination*—we pray at the center of the labyrinth, the heart of God; (3) *union*—as we walk out of the labyrinth, we bring into union the details of life and the illumination found at the center. I have found that the physical movement, the prayer, the clear path, and walking with other pilgrims bring peace and calm, clarity and rejuvenation.

The most difficult step for me to make is the one step that will take me out of the labyrinth. In the process of walking, this path marked on a floor canvas becomes a haven in the midst of my world. During the thirty minutes I spend walking, it's as if walls build themselves between me and the world, walls that shelter me from the storms of my life and shut out chaos, allowing my mind to become clear.

As I come to the edge of the labyrinth, ready to step back into the world, I feel as hesitant to leave it as I would to leave the embrace of a loved one. I have been held, loved, comforted; yet I feel God nudging me out of the labyrinth and back into the world. The illumination I have found is not for my personal gain but to make me more compassionate, faithful, and effective in the world.

DON'T WORRY ABOUT YOUR SHOES

Day 3 Exercise

READ MARK 10:17-22.

REFLECT Traveling in the spirit of Christ means traveling light, unlike the rich man in this story who wanted to inherit eternal life but was unable to follow Jesus.

What areas of your life have you closed off to God's call? Check out the parts of your life you consider "good" or "successful." Where do you fear God's disturbing what you have for the sake of the life God wants you to inherit? Meditate on Jesus' words, "You lack one thing." What would Jesus say to you?

PRAY In prayer, risk placing your whole life in God's hands, including all your achievements. Rest in the assurance that God loves you and knows all that you are and can be.

ACT As a step toward simplicity, today choose an item from your room to give away to someone who needs it more than you do.

Day 3 Reading

Methodism founder John Wesley was known for saying that a person with two pairs of shoes had one pair too many. Yet, I still think it's important to have at least two pairs of black shoes alone. And that's in addition to the essential pair of tennis shoes, flip-flops, and Birkenstocks—they will last forever, right? When I pack for a trip—a weekend or two weeks—it is agony not to take all these shoes with me. For all my good intentions and rhetoric about social justice, I keep buying shoes!

Author and teacher Eugene Peterson renders Jesus' instructions to "his twelve harvest hands" (Matt. 10:5) this way:

> Don't think you have to put on a fund-raising campaign before you start. You don't need a lot of equipment. *You* are the equipment, and all you need to keep that going is three meals a day. Travel light.
>
> When you enter a town or village, don't insist on staying in a luxury inn. Get a modest place with some modest people, and be content there until you leave (Matt. 10:9-11, THE MESSAGE)

In the New Revised Standard Version of that text, Jesus instructs the disciples not even to take one pair of sandals. Travel light, he says, because *you* are the equipment necessary for the journey. It is practical advice for an overpacker like me—and sage advice for anyone in our consumer society. Despite the messages from every television commercial, magazine ad, billboard, and airbrush-perfect celebrity, our value lies in who we are, the decisions we make, and the spirit with which we live our lives—not our clothes, hairstyle, cologne, or even shoes.

We are each sent out into the world just like the first twelve disciples. We are to go to the lost, the confused, the sick, the marginalized, and the imprisoned. And we do not need to take a lot of stuff with us.

The people we meet on our journey need to hear good news of love and compassion, mercy and justice. I think Jesus and John Wesley knew that it is a lot easier to believe and convey the good news if you're not worried about your shoes!

BECOMING WHO GOD CREATED YOU TO BE

Day 4 Exercise

READ 2 CORINTHIANS 1:3-7.

REFLECT In order to become fully who God created us to be, we need to let God use all our experiences as means of grace for others, even our sufferings. In these verses, Paul writes that God comforts us in our difficulties so that we can do the same for others.

Think of a past wound or hurt that has enabled you to feel compassion for those who face similar challenges. How did you experience God's consolation or call in the midst of your distress? How is God calling you to use your experience for the sake of others? In what way might doing so help you to become all God created you to be?

PRAY In prayer, offer your hurts or other negative experiences to God for healing—and for the sake of those you might be able to help.

ACT Go to someone who suffers a pain you have suffered. Listen and share.

Day 4 Reading

I have found that the most difficult part of parenting is allowing my daughter to develop the personality and gifts God has given her without manipulating her, encouraging her to conform, or pushing her to be something she is not. For example, kids today sense a great deal of pressure to be bold, courageous, and involved in sports. So, when my daughter was three years old we tried gymnastics. She was afraid to go upside down. When she was four, I asked her if she wanted to play soccer. She politely said, "No. It sounds like a lot of work." At five she got a scooter for her birthday. Instead of chasing after the neighborhood kids at breakneck speed, she moved slowly and cautiously, one small push at a time, around the cul-de-sac. And she is not one of those kids who will play outside until we make her come in. I'll hear the backdoor open, and my daughter will inform me that she just needs some time by herself. Up she'll go to her room to color or look at her books.

It would be so easy to keep enrolling her in sports, pushing her to "try harder." It is tough to bite my tongue as other kids ride circles around her on their scooters. But as a good partner, my husband points out that she is perfectly content. God has given her the gift of a strong will that allows her to speak up for what she wants and doesn't want. She possesses the gift of patience that allows her to learn skills at her own pace, with fewer injuries and thus more confidence in her abilities. She often prefers books and silence to a game of tag and lots of friends in the backyard.

If I were to push her to be like the other kids or to "just do it," I would be stifling the amazing and unique person God has created her to be. I am her parent, entrusted with God's child to love and nurture. My job is not to get in the way of the perfect individual God envisions her to be.

And so I hope that I have the same patience with others who are learning and becoming who God created them to be. And I pray that others will have patience with me as I fumble around trying to be all that God has created me to be.

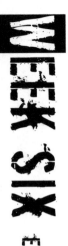
LIVING WITH GOD MOMENT BY MOMENT

Day 5 Exercise

READ COLOSSIANS 3:12-17.

REFLECT God calls us to a way of living every moment of our lives in the spirit of Christ. This passage expresses the spirit of what some call the Christ-style, which is marked by gratitude.

What do you see here in this passage that expresses the life you want to live or the kind of person you want to be?

Reflect on your experience in *The Way of Pilgrimage*. What are you most thankful for? What has helped you most toward becoming the person God calls you to be and that you want to be?

PRAY Bring to mind your group and your pilgrimage together "and be thankful."

ACT "Whatever you do, in word or deed, do everything in the name of the Lord Jesus, giving thanks to God the Father through him" (Col. 3:17).

Day 5 Reading

Each of you has a unique story that began at the moment of your birth, and you have a unique calling that may or may not yet be clear to you. You have so many gifts to offer and abilities still to discover. You have committed to your faith growth and spiritual formation. And you have the potential to look at life with hope and confidence. This does not insure your success in every endeavor or a life without trials. But you are poised to embark on a new stage of your life, equipped with new insights and spiritual practices.

In each and every moment—every time you inhale, exhale, or blink—you can open yourself to the movement of the Holy Spirit and see the vision of creation that God holds. And in each and every moment you can choose to ignore or depart from God's gentle leading.

As you strive to discern and faithfully follow your vocation, God offers a life guided by hope and sustained by grace. Yes, you bear the repercussions of your actions, good and bad. Yes, you bear the responsibility to make further choices that are healthy for you and beneficial to the world, contributing to the coming reign of God. But you also have the opportunity, in every moment, to hear and follow the promptings of the Holy Spirit. It doesn't matter if you have never sought God's call, if you have been actively ignoring Jesus' message, or if you have made some wrong turns. In this moment . . . and this one . . . and this one . . .you can begin to follow and live your spiritual vocation in the world.

As you step out into the world, remember that your vocation is a moment-by-moment, breath-by-breath series of opportunities and choices. God has created you perfectly for participation in this crazy world. God has created you for relationship with folks around you trying to live as best they can moment-by-moment. And God will be faithful to you no matter where your pilgrimage takes you. So be bold, step out, and seek God with all that you are. And remember, the risen Christ is willing to be your constant traveling companion.

WHICH GIFTS DO YOU HAVE?

Self-Assessment Inventory

Instructions: For each of the 75 questions that follow, circle the number that corresponds with the response that most closely matches how you perceive yourself. Circle 4 if the statement is very true; 3, frequently true; 2, sometimes true; 1, infrequently true; 0 if rarely true. You might also ask a friend to score the inventory with, and for, you. Your friend's perception of your strengths may be useful in identifying the gifts with which you have been amply blessed. After responding to each question, turn to the scoring grid on page 76 to discover your results. If you would like to take this Inventory online, go to www.elca.org/youth/resource/inventory.html.

	Very true of me	Frequently true of me	Sometimes true of me	Infrequently true of me	Rarely true of me
1. When presented a goal, I quickly think of what to do to achieve the desired result.	4	3	2	1	0
2. I express myself through artistic means.	4	3	2	1	0
3. My faith makes me seek out God's will and purpose in the circumstances of my daily life.	4	3	2	1	0
4. I am able to talk with those who do not go to church about God in ways they are able to easily understand.	4	3	2	1	0
5. I am moved by those who, through conflict or sorrow, are doubting God's presence in their lives.	4	3	2	1	0
6. I often see the Holy Spirit's presence in my life and the lives of others.	4	3	2	1	0
7. God blesses me each day. I tend to gladly respond to these blessings by giving generously of my time and money.	4	3	2	1	0
8. When I see a new youth visit our congregation, I introduce myself and help that person feel welcome.	4	3	2	1	0
9. I know that God hears and answers my daily prayers.	4	3	2	1	0
10. I want to learn as much as I can about the Bible and faith.	4	3	2	1	0
11. I am a take-charge person. With others' help, I know the goal or task will be completed.	4	3	2	1	0
12. When I see someone in need, I want to assist the person.	4	3	2	1	0
13. I love to dance and enjoy encouraging others through movement.	4	3	2	1	0
14. I find joy in expressing myself by playing a musical instrument or by singing.	4	3	2	1	0
15. I am able to encourage others to develop in their faith.	4	3	2	1	0
16. I like working behind the scenes to make sure projects are successful.	4	3	2	1	0
17. I enjoy working with my hands in a skill that requires considerable experience to perfect.	4	3	2	1	0
18. I love to tell others about biblical truth in a way that it becomes real to them.	4	3	2	1	0
19. When a challenge is presented, I am usually able to identify a workable solution.	4	3	2	1	0
20. I am able to take a thought or idea and put it into a clear and inspiring written form.	4	3	2	1	0

Circle 4 if the statement is very true; 3, frequently true; 2, sometimes true; 1, infrequently true; 0 if rarely true.

	Very true of me	Frequently true of me	Sometimes true of me	Infrequently true of me	Rarely true of me
21. I am very comfortable using computers to organize information.	4	3	2	1	0
22. I feel compelled to speak up for people who cannot defend themselves.	4	3	2	1	0
23. I enjoy friendships with people much older or much younger than myself.	4	3	2	1	0
24. People have told me they appreciate my listening when they have a personal challenge.	4	3	2	1	0
25. I love to act out stories from the Bible.	4	3	2	1	0
26. I enjoy organizing thoughts, ideas, hopes, and dreams into a specific plan of action.	4	3	2	1	0
27. I can translate into an artistic form what I first see in my imagination.	4	3	2	1	0
28. I have helped others figure out which personal decisions help them live God's will for their lives.	4	3	2	1	0
29. I enjoy being with others not involved in church and like having the opportunity to encourage them to faith and commitment in God.	4	3	2	1	0
30. When someone faces a crisis, I am compelled to show my care and support.	4	3	2	1	0
31. I have told others of the Spirit's presence in times of my own personal crises, to be a source of strength for them.	4	3	2	1	0
32. I manage my time and money so that I can give much of it to the work of the church or other organizations.	4	3	2	1	0
33. I love when others come to my house to hang out, even if there are some I don't know very well.	4	3	2	1	0
34. I can become so involved in prayer that outside distractions don't bother me.	4	3	2	1	0
35. I often study something in the Bible and think about how it influences my daily life.	4	3	2	1	0
36. In a group, others often look to me for direction.	4	3	2	1	0
37. I feel compelled to do what I can to provide housing for the homeless, food for the starving, comfort for those in distress.	4	3	2	1	0
38. When I dance before groups, I feel a real sense of God's presence.	4	3	2	1	0
39. I am inspired and provide inspiration for others by my singing or playing a musical instrument.	4	3	2	1	0
40. I have taken responsibility to provide spiritual guidance to an individual believer or group of believers.	4	3	2	1	0
41. People tell me that without my willingness to do the unnoticed jobs, their work would be more difficult.	4	3	2	1	0
42. I am good at building, repairing, or restoring things and find satisfaction in doing so.	4	3	2	1	0
43. I want to express my faith by helping others discover the truths in the Bible.	4	3	2	1	0

Circle 4 if the statement is very true; 3, frequently true; 2, sometimes true; 1, infrequently true; 0 if rarely true.

	Very true of me	Frequently true of me	Sometimes true of me	Infrequently true of me	Rarely true of me
44. People come to me for help in applying Christian faith and values to personal situations.	4	3	2	1	0
45. I often feel moved to write about my thoughts and feelings so others may benefit from them.	4	3	2	1	0
46. I see the Internet as a great place to communicate and share my faith with others.	4	3	2	1	0
47. I try to find a way through the system for people who are unable to get through it on their own.	4	3	2	1	0
48. I am eager to learn from people older or younger than myself—and like to share what I know with them.	4	3	2	1	0
49. I could listen to people's stories for hours.	4	3	2	1	0
50. When I am acting on stage, I feel a real sense of God's presence.	4	3	2	1	0
51. I have been successful in organizing, directing, and motivating people to achieve a goal.	4	3	2	1	0
52. My artistic work helps others think about God.	4	3	2	1	0
53. In my congregation, I often get a gut feeling if a direction being taken is in line with God's will and purpose.	4	3	2	1	0
54. I do not find it difficult to share what Jesus means to me with my friends.	4	3	2	1	0
55. Those seeking answers for life's questions have come to me for encouragement.	4	3	2	1	0
56. I can see great things happening in my congregation, even when others are doubtful.	4	3	2	1	0
57. When I receive money unexpectedly, I want to share this gift with the church.	4	3	2	1	0
58. I enjoy welcoming guests and helping them to feel at ease in new situations.	4	3	2	1	0
59. Others have asked me to pray for them in difficult times.	4	3	2	1	0
60. I usually know of something in the Bible to help others on their faith journey.	4	3	2	1	0
61. People say they like to work with me because the task will be successfully completed.	4	3	2	1	0
62. People have been surprised by my comfort in working with those suffering in mind, body, or spirit.	4	3	2	1	0
63. I am often amazed that my dancing provides inspiration and hope for others on their faith journey.	4	3	2	1	0
64. Others have told me they were moved by my playing a musical instrument or by singing.	4	3	2	1	0
65. Friends have come to me for spiritual help, and it has deepened our relationship.	4	3	2	1	0
66. At church, when I help take down tables, work in the kitchen, put chairs away or fold bulletins, I feel that I have served the Lord.	4	3	2	1	0

Circle 4 if the statement is very true; 3, frequently true; 2, sometimes true; 1, infrequently true and 0 if rarely true.

	Very true of me	Frequently true of me	Sometimes true of me	Infrequently true of me	Rarely true of me
67. My knowledge of building, maintenance, or repair has been of special value to the church and others.	4	3	2	1	0
68. Others have told me that I can take the most difficult idea or concept and help them understand it.	4	3	2	1	0
69. When a group's direction is needed, I am frequently asked for my opinion.	4	3	2	1	0
70. My written work has helped others understand life's truths.	4	3	2	1	0
71. I have used technology (computers, communications) to help others deal with life and grow in their faith.	4	3	2	1	0
72. I do whatever I can to get those in power to address the needs of the homeless, the hungry, or the excluded.	4	3	2	1	0
73. I have friends who are at least 10 years older or younger than I.	4	3	2	1	0
74. I always have time to hear about my friends' joys and sorrows.	4	3	2	1	0
75. My abilities as an actress/actor have had special value to the church and others.	4	3	2	1	0

SCORING GRID

For each set of three questions, below left, fill in the number of rectangular blocks equal to your total score. For example, in the illustration to the right, in the category of Administration, the numbers $2 + 4 + 3$ total 9. The strongest gifts will generally have a total score of "7" or more. If you have more than one gift with a total of seven or more, then all of these gifts can be referred to as your "gift cluster." In the illustration, the gifts of Administration, Encouragement, Faith, Knowledge, and Leadership are the gift cluster. Notice how each gift within the cluster has potential to complement and support another. This inventory is not a scientific instrument, but it is designed to begin your journey toward spiritual gifts discovery.

	0	1	2	3	4	5	6	7	8	9	10	11	12	
														Administration
														Discernment
														Evangelism
														Encouragement
														Faith
														Giving
														Hospitality
														Intercession
														Knowledge
														Leadership
														Mercy
														Pastoring
														Service
														Teaching
														Wisdom

SPIRITUAL GIFTS

	0	1	2	3	4	5	6	7	8	9	10	11	12	
Questions 1, 26, 51														Administration
Questions 3, 28, 53														Discernment
Questions 4, 29, 54														Evangelism
Questions 5, 30, 55														Encouragement
Questions 6, 31, 56														Faith
Questions 7, 32, 57														Giving
Questions 8, 33, 58														Hospitality
Questions 9, 34, 59														Intercession
Questions 10, 35, 60														Knowledge
Questions 11, 36, 61														Leadership
Questions 12, 37, 62														Mercy
Questions 15, 40, 65														Pastoring
Questions 16, 41, 66														Service
Questions 18, 43, 68														Teaching
Questions 19, 44, 69														Wisdom

RELATIONAL GIFTS

	0	1	2	3	4	5	6	7	8	9	10	11	12	
Questions 22, 47, 72														Advocacy
Questions 2, 27, 52														Artistry
Questions 13, 38, 63														Dance
Questions 25, 50, 75														Drama
Questions 23, 48, 73														Intergenerational Openness
Questions 24, 49, 74														Listening
Questions 14, 39, 64														Music
Questions 17, 42, 67														Skilled Craft
Questions 21, 46, 71														Technological Skill
Questions 20, 45, 70														Writing

GIFT CLUSTER

In each of the large circles to the right, write one of the spiritual gifts that had a total score of seven or more. Begin with the center circle, identifying the gift with the highest score. In the event of a tie, select the gift with which you feel more comfortable. Then fill the other large circles with up to five of the remaining gifts. Use the small circles to record your relational gifts. This group of gifts is your gift cluster.

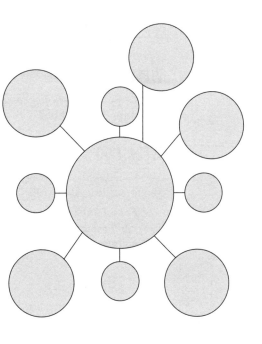

NOTES

INTRODUCTION

1. T. S. Eliot, "Little Gidding" Part V, in Four Quartets, in *T. S. Eliot: The Complete Poems and Plays 1909–1950* (New York: Harcourt Brace Jovanovich, 1971), 145.

WEEK ONE

1. Phillips Brooks, quoted at http://www.brainyquote.com/quotes/authors/p/phillips_brooks.html

WEEK TWO

1. Quoted in *Among Friends* newsletter (Edinburgh: Europe and Middle East Section of Friends World Committee for Consultation), No. 94: Spring 2004.

2. N. Graham Standish, "Humility," in *The Upper Room Dictionary of Christian Spiritual Formation,* ed. Keith Beasley-Topliffe (Nashville: Tenn.: Upper Room Books, 2003), 136–37.

WEEK THREE

1. Frederick Buechner, *Wishful Thinking: A Seeker's ABC,* rev. ed. (San Francisco: HarperSanFrancisco, 1993), 65.

WEEK FOUR

1. Buechner, *Wishful Thinking,* 137.

WEEK FIVE

1. Peter John Mayer, "Story of My Life," CD recording *Straw House Down* (New Brighton, Minn.: Peppermint Records). Lyrics available at www.blueboat.net.

2. Lindsay Morgan, "Hungering for Justice: A Student Hunger Strike Brings Support to Low-Income Workers," *Sojourners* (June 2005):9.

3. Gayle Turner Watson, *Guide for Covenant Discipleship Groups* (Nashville, Tenn.: Discipleship Resources, 2000), 75.

4. Frederick Buechner, *The Sacred Journey: A Memoir of Early Days* (San Francisco: HarperSanFrancisco, 1991), 107.

WEEK SIX

1. Madeleine L'Engle, "Three Days," in *The Ordering of Love: The New and Collected Poems of Madeleine L'Engle* (Colorado Springs, Colo.: WaterBrook Press 2005), 271.

JOURNAL PAGE

JOURNAL PAGE